A Note for Parents and Caregivers

This book is not a lesson in definitions.

It will not teach children "the right meaning" of words, nor will it train them to win arguments about language. That is deliberate.

Plato's Cratylus is a dialogue about a question children already live with every day, often without naming   it:

Do   words   really   fit   what   they   name? And if they do—how?

Children   argue   about   words   constantly. "It's   not   fair."

"That's   not   what   I   meant."

"You're using that wrong."

Plato   noticed   this   too.   He   understood   that disagreements   about   words   are   rarely   about vocabulary   alone.   They   are   about   shared understanding—about whether we are still standing on the same ground when we speak.

This book invites children into that question gently.

Plato	does	not	lecture.
He			walks.
He	tests	ideas	aloud.
He			hesitates.

He returns.

The children in the story never receive full explanations. They overhear fragments. They misunderstand. They try again. This mirrors real learning far better than polished answers. Understanding grows by return, not by conclusion.

As an adult reader, you may notice that this book resists closure. It does not tell children what to think about language. Instead, it helps them develop habits:

- listening for how words are used
- noticing when meanings drift
- holding differences without forcing agreement

- returning to shared words with care

You do not need to explain the philosophy while reading. In fact, it is often better not to. Let the pauses remain pauses. Let the questions stay open.

If a child asks, "So what's the answer?"

A good response is:

"Let's walk the question again."

That is how Plato taught.

That is how this book is meant to be used.

The path is still there.

Do Names Belong to Things?

1. Letter to the Reader

You may think a name is just a sound.

Something we agree to say so we can point and move on.

Plato does not move on so quickly.

He wonders whether names merely happen—or whether they fit.

Whether they drift like leaves—or hold like knots.

In this book, Plato does not argue from a podium.

He walks.

He speaks aloud.

A scribe follows, trying to keep pace.

And three children sit beneath an olive tree, catching only pieces.

You will not be told what to think.

You will be invited to notice.

You may feel, at times, that Plato circles without arriving.

That is not a mistake.

Some questions are learned by return.

---

2. The First Circuit

Plato walks the circular path slowly.

"Names," he says, "are small things that carry large weight."

The scribe writes quickly.

"Some say a name belongs to a thing by nature," Plato continues.

"Others say it belongs by agreement."

He stops.

Looks at the ground where the path has been worn smooth.

"Two sides," he says.

"One pulls toward fixed truth.

The other toward free choice."

The   scribe   hesitates.

Plato walks on.

---

3. The Spoken Account — First Pass

"Imagine," Plato says, "a tool."

"A hammer?" the scribe asks.

"Yes. Or a shuttle. Or a rudder."

Plato   gestures   toward   the   path's   edge.

Loose stones. Packed earth.

"A   tool   works   when   it   fits   its   task.

Not   every   shape   cuts.

Not every sound guides."

He pauses.

"A name is also a tool."

The scribe looks up.

"It   teaches.

It   separates.

It lets us speak together."

Plato resumes walking.

"If names were only whatever anyone wished, speech would scatter."

---

4. The Spoken Account — Second Pass

"But if names were perfectly fixed," Plato says, "we would stop listening."

He bends, picks up a leaf.

"This leaf has edges. If there were only one edge, it would tear. If there were no edge, it would dissolve."

He drops it.

"Two sides pull apart. The middle lets them belong."

The scribe writes, then stops.

"I am writing," the scribe says, "but I don't yet know what I'm writing."

Plato smiles.

"Good. Then you're still thinking."

---

5. The Spoken Account — Third Pass

"Those who first gave names," Plato says, "were not careless."

"They   listened.

They   measured.

They shaped sound toward meaning."

He looks toward the olive tree.

"But even the best name must be used well."

"A dialec—" the scribe begins.

"A   questioner,"   Plato   says   gently.

"One who tests, not owns."

They complete the circuit.

---

6. Between the Columns — Under the Olive Tree

Theo   tilts   his   head.

"So... names pull two ways?"

Mira   presses   her   fingers   into   the   dirt.

"Maybe the name holds the thing... like a string holds a note."

Leo   frowns.

"But people still argue about names."

They fall quiet as Plato passes again.

---

7. The Last Circuit

Plato slows.

"A   name   can   miss,"   he   says.

"And still point."

"It   can   fit   imperfectly,

and still teach."

He stops walking.

"The danger is not wrong names," he says.

"It is refusing to test them together."

---

8. ☐ Under the Olive Tree — Let's Talk

- Have you ever noticed a name that felt right—or

  wrong?

- Can two people use the same word and mean

  different things?

- What happens when no one checks how a word is being used?

- Where do you see two sides pulling apart—and something holding between them?

---

9. ⬜ Learn Like Plato!

Greek word: onoma — name

Plato treats names as tools for shared thinking, not labels.

Try   this:

Ask your AI assistant to explain a word you use often.

Then ask it to explain the same word in a different way.

Notice what stayed the same—and what changed.

Thinking lives in the middle.

Do Names Move When Things Move?

1. Letter to the Reader

In the first walk, Plato asked whether names belong to things—or only to agreement.

Now he asks something harder.

If a thing is never still, can a name ever stay?

Some people say the world flows like a river. Others say it stands like a stone.

If both speak, how do we listen?

This book does not answer that question. It stretches it.

You may feel the ground widen under your feet. You may feel less certain where the middle lies.

That, too, is part of learning.

2. The First Circuit

The   path   is   wider   here.

The stones are farther apart.

Plato walks more slowly.

"Some," he says, "claim all things move."

The scribe writes.

"Others say what truly is does not."

Plato stops at a place where water crosses the path after rain.

"If   everything   moves,"   he   says,

"speech must chase."

"If   nothing   moves,"

"speech freezes."

He steps over the water.

---

3. The Spoken Account — First Pass

"Imagine a river," Plato says.

The scribe looks up.

"You cannot step into the same water twice."

Plato nods.

"If   this   is   so,"   he   continues,

"what does a name do?"

"Does   it   move   with   the   water?"

"Or does it point from the bank?"

He pauses.

"If   it   moves   too   quickly,

it loses grip."

"If   it   does   not   move   at   all,

it misses the flow."

The scribe underlines misses.

---

4. The Spoken Account — Second Pass

Plato gestures to the path.

"See   how   it   curves,"   he   says.

"It returns, but never exactly."

"Motion   does   not   destroy   sameness.

Sameness does not cancel motion."

He presses his foot into the earth.

"A tuned string holds tension."

"Too   loose—no   sound."

"Too tight—it snaps."

He looks at the scribe.

"Names are tuned."

The scribe hesitates.

"I   am   writing,"   he   says,

"but the words keep sliding."

Plato smiles.

"Good. Then you are following the motion."

---

5. The Spoken Account — Third Pass

"Those   who   say   only   motion,"   Plato   says,

"cannot explain learning."

"If   everything   changes   entirely,

nothing is recognized."

"But those who say only stillness," he continues,

"cannot explain error."

"If names never move, why do we correct them?"

He resumes walking.

"Two pulls," he says.

"One toward flow.

One toward form."

"The middle lets speech remain possible."

---

6. Between the Columns — Under the Olive Tree

Theo squints.

"So... words move, but not too much?"

Mira hums softly.

"Like a song that stays the same even when you sing it again."

Leo kicks a pebble.

"If everything changes, how do we know anything?"

They look up.

Plato is already past.

---

7. The Last Circuit

Plato slows near the widest part of the path.

"To speak," he says,

"is to aim while moving."

"A name must be steady enough to return,

and flexible enough to follow."

He stops.

"When either is lost,

shared speech breaks."

---

8. ☐ Under the Olive Tree — Let's Talk

- Have you noticed words that changed meaning over time?

- Can something stay the same while also changing?

- When do fixed words help—and when do they get in the way?

- Where do you see motion needing measure in your own speaking?

9. ⬚ Learn Like Plato!

Greek word: kinesis — motion

Plato listens for how movement and sameness belong together.

Try   this:

Ask your AI assistant to explain a word as if it never changes.

Then ask it to explain the same word as if it is always changing.

Notice where each explanation helps—and where it fails.

The middle is where thinking stays alive.

Do Names Look Upward?

1. Letter to the Reader

So far, Plato has walked close to the ground.

He asked whether names fit.

Then whether they move.

Now his gaze lifts.

Some names seem to point beyond what we can touch.

They do not only follow things.

They seem to lead.

This book asks whether names can aim higher than what is changing—

and whether such aiming helps us speak together, or tempts us to drift away from what we see.

You may feel the walk open.

You may feel the ground thin.

That is where this question lives.

2. The First Circuit

The path slopes slightly upward.

Plato walks with his head raised.

"Some   names,"   he   says,

"are not given to things we can hold."

The scribe writes.

"They are given to what we look toward."

He stops and points to the sky between the branches.

"The   sun   does   not   argue.

Yet we orient by it."

3. The Spoken Account — First Pass

"Think of direction," Plato says.

"A   ship   at   sea   moves," he   continues,

"but not without a bearing."

He traces a line in the air.

"If   names   only   follow   motion,

they wander."

"If names only repeat what we see, they never guide."

He pauses.

"Some names lift our sight."

The scribe looks up from the page.

---

4. The Spoken Account — Second Pass

"Consider how we name the sky," Plato says.

"We do not grasp it. We look."

"And yet," he adds, "we speak as if it holds."

He slows his steps.

"To look upward is not to escape the ground. It is to find direction while standing on it."

He glances at the scribe.

"A name that only floats loses use."

"A name that never lifts loses aim."

The path curves higher.

5. The Spoken Account — Third Pass

"Those who claim names come only from below,"

Plato   says,

"cannot explain why we return to certain words."

"And those who claim names come only from above,"

"forget how easily speech loses touch."

He stops walking.

"Two   pulls   again,"   he   says.

"One   toward   what   appears.

One toward what guides."

"The middle lets us speak without blindness."

The scribe hesitates, pen hovering.

"I   am   writing,"   he   says,

"but the page feels farther away."

Plato smiles.

"Good. Then your sight has lifted."

6. Between the Columns — Under the Olive Tree

Theo shades his eyes.

"Are names like stars?"

Mira tilts her head back.

"Maybe they help us not get lost."

Leo squints upward, then down.

"But stars don't tell us where to step."

They fall silent.

---

7. The Last Circuit

The highest point of the path is quiet.

"To name," Plato says,

"is not only to follow."

"It is also to orient."

He looks once more at the sky.

"When names forget the ground,

they become dreams."

"When they forget direction,

they become noise."

He turns back toward the path's descent.

8. ⬚ Under the Olive Tree — Let's Talk

- Have you noticed words that seem to point beyond what you can see?

- When do guiding words help—and when do they mislead?

- Can something give direction without giving instructions?

- Where do you look when you are unsure how to speak?

9. ⬚ Learn Like Plato!

Greek word: horos — boundary, limit, horizon

Plato listens for how looking up still needs limits.

Try   this:

Ask your AI assistant to explain a big idea in very simple   words.

Then ask it to explain the same idea as something you can   only   point   toward.

Notice which explanation helps you orient—and which one loses you.

Thinking needs direction and ground.

Do Names Still Work When We Stop Speaking?

1. Letter to the Reader

So far, Plato has kept moving.

He tested names by how they fit things.

Then by how they move with change.

Then by how they guide our sight.

Now he slows.

This book asks what happens when speech hesitates—

when we stop trying to guide, explain, or point.

Some words fall apart when we pause.

Others remain.

This is not because they are louder.

It is because they are held differently.

This book listens more than it speaks.

2. The First Circuit

The path narrows again.

Plato walks quietly.

After a long moment, he speaks.

"When we stop speaking," he says, "names do not vanish."

The scribe waits before writing.

"They remain," Plato continues, "as echoes."

He touches his chest lightly.

"Some words still sound even when the mouth is closed."

3. The Spoken Account — First Pass

"Consider silence," Plato says.

"Not the silence that interrupts," "but the silence that holds."

He takes a slower step.

"When speech rushes, names are pushed."

"When speech rests, names show their weight."

He pauses.

"Some names collapse when unattended."

"Others stay."

The scribe writes fewer words.

---

4. The Spoken Account — Second Pass

"Think of memory," Plato says.

"Not remembering facts— remembering sense."

He looks down at the path.

"A word you have used carelessly disappears."

"A word you have tested returns."

He stops walking.

"The middle is not always movement."

"Sometimes it is restraint."

The scribe looks up.

"I   am   writing,"   he   says   slowly,

"but nothing is happening."

Plato nods.

"Good. Then something is settling."

---

5. The Spoken Account — Third Pass

"Those who speak without pause," Plato says,

"do not hear what their words do."

"And   those   who   never   speak,"

"cannot test what remains."

He resumes walking, gently.

"Two   dangers,"   he   says.

"One   is   noise.

One is withdrawal."

"The middle lets speech rest without disappearing."

---

6. Between the Columns — Under the Olive Tree

Theo whispers.

"Why did he stop talking?"

Mira closes her eyes.

"It feels like the words stayed."

Leo frowns.

"But how do you check a word if no one says it?"

They listen.

---

7. The Last Circuit

Plato completes the loop slowly.

"A name," he says,

"is not only a sound."

"It is also a habit of attention."

He stops.

"When attention scatters,

names flatten."

"When attention holds,

names deepen."

He turns back toward the path.

8. ☐ Under the Olive Tree — Let's Talk

- Have you noticed words that feel different when you say them quietly?

- Are there words that stay with you even when no one is speaking?

- When does silence help you understand a word better?

- What happens when speech never pauses?

9. ☐ Learn Like Plato!

Greek word: logos — word, account, gathered sense

Plato treats logos as something that gathers meaning, not rushes it.

Try   this:

Ask your AI assistant to explain an idea briefly.

Then   wait   before   responding.

Ask   it   again,   using   fewer   words.

Notice what remains.

Thinking sometimes happens when speech rests.

How Do Names Stay Shared?

1. Letter to the Reader

Plato has walked far.

He has tested names by how they fit things.

By how they move with change.

By how they guide our sight.

By how they remain when speech pauses.

Now he asks one last question.

How do names stay shared?

Not   owned.

Not   frozen.

Not drifting.

Shared.

This book does not close the question of names.

It steadies it.

---

2. The First Circuit

The path is familiar again.

Plato's steps are even.

"When people speak together," he says,

"they do not all mean the same thing."

The scribe writes.

"And yet," Plato continues,

"they understand enough."

He gestures to the packed earth between stones.

"This is not chance."

---

3. The Spoken Account — First Pass

"Consider measure," Plato says.

"Not counting.

Not rules."

He presses his foot into the path.

"Measure is what lets difference belong."

"If names were private,"

"they would scatter."

"If   names   were   fixed   beyond   use,"

"they would break."

He pauses.

"What   holds   is   not   sameness."

"It is proportion."

---

4. The Spoken Account — Second Pass

"Those who demand perfect names," Plato says,

"silence conversation."

"And   those   who   accept   any   name,"

"lose meaning."

He looks toward the olive tree.

"Between them is care."

"A shared word survives because people return to it—
and adjust."

The scribe slows his writing.

"I   am   writing,"   he   says,

"and this time I know what I am writing."

Plato smiles.

"Good. Then you are ready to stop."

---

5. The Spoken Account — Third Pass

"A   name,"   Plato   says,

"is a meeting place."

"It gathers use, motion, direction, and pause."

He stops walking.

"When   people   test   words   together,

names hold."

"When   they   refuse   to   test   them,

names harden or dissolve."

He resumes, steady.

"The   middle   is   not   compromise."

"It is shared attention."

---

6. Between the Columns — Under the Olive Tree

Theo   nods   slowly.

"So words work because we keep checking them?"

Mira   smiles.

"Because we care how they fit together."

Leo   shrugs.

"So... words don't win. People do—or don't."

They sit quietly.

---

7. The Last Circuit

Plato completes the circle.

"A   name,"   he   says,

"lasts when it can be returned to."

"Not   because   it   is   perfect."

"But because it is held."

He stops near where he began.

"That is enough for now."

---

8. ☐ Under the Olive Tree — Let's Talk

- What words do you share with others that
  matter to you?

- How do you notice when a shared word starts to drift?

- What helps a conversation stay together over time?

- Where do you see measure—not extremes—holding things in place?

---

9. ⬜ Learn Like Plato!

Greek word: metron — measure

For Plato, measure is what lets many hold one thing together.

Try   this:

Ask your AI assistant to explain a word you care about.

Then ask it how someone else might use the same word   differently.

Finally, ask what must stay the same for the word to remain shared.

Thinking lives where return is possible.

After the Walk

The path is quiet now.

The olive tree still stands at the center.

The stones have not moved.

The words have not disappeared.

Plato does not announce an ending.

He never does.

A name, he has shown, is not a thing you finish with.

It is something you return to.

You may have hoped, at some point, that he would decide:

whether names belong to nature

or to agreement

or to motion

or to thought.

He did not.

Instead, he showed what happens when people keep testing words together.

Names fail when they are treated as possessions.

They fail when they are treated as noise.

They fail when they are lifted too far from use or pressed too hard into certainty.

They endure when they are held with care.

Not   frozen.

Not   drifting.

Held.

The children under the tree did not receive answers.

They   received   habits:

listening,

checking,

returning.

The   scribe   did   not   master   the   words.

He learned when to stop writing.

And   Plato—

Plato simply walked.

If you find yourself arguing about words, return to the middle.

If a word feels empty, test it.

If it feels rigid, listen again.

That is not how philosophy ends. That is how it stays alive.

The path remains. You may walk it again.

www.ingramcontent.com/pod-product-compliance
Lightning Source LLC
Chambersburg PA
CBHW081644040426
42449CB00015B/3455